Matthew Gray

Shopify

A Simple Step-by-Step Guide for Beginners to Start your Online E-Commerce Business by Shopify Stores

E - COMMERCE

Table of Contents

Introduction

The simplest way to create an e-commerce business for yourself is by using Shopify. Shopify is an all-round e-commerce solution for businesses that wish to sell their products on-line. So, you don't need any massive capital or investments to start your business. All that you need is a good idea and a reliable Internet connection. Also, you don't need any technical knowledge to create an e-commerce website. If theimpression of creating a website seems daunting, don't worry because you aren't alone. Plenty of people feel this way before they realize how simple Shopify is. Shopify simplifies your work, and it takes less than 20 minutes to create a skeletal framework of your e-commerce store on Shopify. Shopify is an incredible and intuitive platform that allows you to personalize your on-line store, sell any products you want, and accept various forms of payment while providing good customer service.

If you are looking for simple setup and a no-hassle shopping cart experience that permits you to focus strongly on your core business functions, then use Shopify. In this book, you will learn all the secrets of starting and maintaining a prosperous on-line retail business using Shopify. Irrespective of you being a small or a medium scale business or you are starting to think of an e-commerce store, Shopify offers a variety of features and benefits. This is ready to use an e-commerce platform. It's specially created for entrepreneurs who aren't well versed in web designing and development. Shopify essentially makes the entire on-line store setup an incredibly easy experience without compromising on the functionality you would expect from a professional e-commerce platform.

In this book, you will learn about Shopify, the benefits it offers, and how to set up an e-commerce store with success. The Shopify store you start can be based on the model of drop-shipping or private labeling. Once you carefully go through all the information given in this book, you will feel confident about starting your own e-commerce store on Shopify.

So, are you eager to learn more about all this? If yes, then let's get started immediately.

Chapter 1: What is Shopify?

Brief Overview:

Initially, Tobias (CEO of Shopify) was fascinated with creating a platform that would help him sell his boards to an on-line buyer.

Lutke and his partner Scott mainly focused on creating an e-commerce platform that was very flexible and easy to use. Shopify was released in 2006, and there was no going back. After a battle of two years, both creators created a new team to turn Shopify into a digital platform we all know and love today. In 2008, Shopify managed to record its first profits and gradually began to recognize itself as an ideal e-commerce platform. Shopify was able to secure additional funding of $ 7 million in 2010 and $ 15 million in funding from 2011. A humble platform that started with the idea of selling snowboards on-line soon grew into a huge e-commerce platform with more than 500,000 e-commerce stores. Shopify is an e-commerce solution that allows store owners to set up their own on-line stores. By using Shopify, you don't need to worry about any issues related to server maintenance, hosting, or branding for clients. The various utilities available can be easily used in Shopify and will help address all of these issues.

Shopify offers many customization options ranging from inventory management, customer usage tracking, on-line store management, or even customer contact. The main goal of Shopify is to help prospective entrepreneurs, and on-line store owners set up their eCommerce stores, even if they don't have the technical knowledge or coding history. All the features that Shopify offers are not only customizable but also incredibly easy to use. So even if you have absolutely zero technical skills, you can easily set up your own on-line store to sell products made by others or your own products. The various challenges associated with designing and launching an eCommerce business are eliminated by using Shopify as a hosting platform.

As we can relate from this brief history, starting an ecommerce business is difficult and involves a lot of risk. A big reason why only a small number of people succeed in such a lucrative business is because getting to the point where your business becomes a success takes a lot of dedication and not a little luck. Shopify exists to help more people looking for a career in ecommerce to reach their goals, with guidance and reduced risk. While creating your own ecommerce website still certainly takes a lot of hard work, Shopify is there to make the process much easier than starting from scratch.

It does this by offering you a baseline to start from when creating your website. It's like a template, allowing you to design a webstore for your business without the need for learning the intricacies of web design or spending precious funds on an expert to use these skills for you. Shopify offers an array of crucial tools pre-designed and ready for use on your webstore, such as theme options to design your site around, shipping and transaction options and translation options so you can sell in multiple countries without the worry of language barriers. It is truly a helpful platform that offers the benefits of owning a webstore to more than just the rich and professional web designers.

Who Uses Shopify?

Shopify is used by tens of thousands of businesses and serves over 2 million customers. Countless products are available, unique to each business, making Shopify a top competitor against many of the top ecommerce platforms in the business.

How Does Shopify Work?

Shopify's platform is divided into two sections:

- The frontend. This is the customer-facing section, the side of Shopify (which includes your webstore) the customers see and can browse at their leisure.
- The backend. This is the section that only you and other webstore owners can see, where you design your site and have the ability to make changes and updates to what the customer sees when necessary. This is where you add new products, edit your design, and specific personalization and customizations to suit your needs (such as social media links).

Through Shopify's platform you can advertise the products you decide to sell. When you're ready, you will be able to organize your products so that customers can find them by specific size, style, color, etc., with ease. Shopify comes with built-in transaction gateway options so you can set your desired prices and immediately watch the customers roll in to buy your products easily online. The platform's easy to-use software makes it possible to have a new product go from simply an idea to having it up and ready to be sold to customers in just a few hours.

Why is Shopify so Useful?

As mentioned before, starting your own ecommerce website is a challenging process. Shopify is a useful tool that allows ecommerce business owners-to-be meet their goals with reduced risk and challenges. It allows you to cut to the chase and start earning money by skipping small (but crucial) steps that can only be avoided by working with a platform like Shopify rather than on your own from scratch. Here are a few examples of what Shopify has to offer for aspiring estore owners.

Website Design

Designing a website is hard work, not just regarding theme and aesthetics but coding and general maintenance as well. When you create a website on your own, assuming you yourself aren't a professional web designer, you would be required to hire such a person before progressing any further toward a thriving business. This can set you back a significant amount when it comes to profit, especially considering you're far from starting to make any income with your business.

Creating a website with Shopify eliminates this hassle because the coding, themes, and maintenance is already taken care of before you even begin building your store. Instead of coding a design yourself, you choose from an array of pre-made options and customize your site to fit your unique desires from there.

Transaction Options

Similarly, embedding a payment system into your website takes a trained programmer in order to set it up securely. This includes ensuring security in the system, as this is your customers' money and financial safety we're talking about, and programming various other necessary features like shipping calculators , which can be tricky if not plain painstaking.

Once again, Shopify already has these features taken care of and can simply be incorporated into your website with a few clicks of a button.

Fulfilling Orders

Shipping out orders from customers takes a lot more than some cardboard boxes with addresses on them, stamps, and a mailbox. In involves more than just you or a small team can do on your own.

Shopify takes care of needs like creating official shipping labels and tasks like working with a dropshipper much less of a challenge than if you were to manage an independent website by yourself.

The Small Details

Shopify takes care of all the little, but crucial, responsibilities that you would have to worry about for the remainder of your career in the market if you were to create your own independent website. This is really what Shopify is all about -- taking care of the small things so you can cut right to the chase, which is focusing solely on your business, its products, and your customers.

Chapter 2: How to Set up Shopify Store

In this section, let us look in detail at all the different steps you must go through to set up an e-commerce store on Shopify.

Step 1: Signing Up

The first step to creating a Shopify e-commerce store is to sign up with Shopify. To do this, visit the official Shopify website and click on the signup form to create an account. Don't forget to click on the "start free trial" button after entering all the required details. Keep in mind that the store name you opt for needs to be unique, or Shopify will prompt you to choose something else. After you enter the email address, you'll be asked to fill out a couple of other personal details like your name, country, address, contact number, alternate email address, and so on. You will also be asked questions about the products you wish to sell, whether you have the said products, and what you want to sell. If you are just going through Shopify to understand how it works, then opt for the, "I'm just playing around" option in the drop-down menu of, "Do you have products?" And select "I am not sure," in the section that asks, "What will you sell?" Once you are satisfied with your answers and have completed all the fields, click on "I am done" to complete the signup process.

Step 2: Log In

Once you have completed the signup process, you can either log out or continue. If you are logged out, log in once again and go toward the store admin screen. Once at the store admin screen, it is time to customize the store, upload products, and set up different forms of payment and shipping.

Step 3: Configuration

Let us look in detail at the different settings that you need to configure while setting up the store. Here are the different steps you must follow while configuring the store to meet your requirements.

Click on the settings menu and select general options.

There are a couple of general details that you can update or change, such as the store details, standards and formats, store currency, and the store address. In the store details, the different information you might have to provide includes an email address to receive any support from Shopify, the store name, and a customer email that all potential customers will see whenever they receive an email from your store. Don't forget to add the legal name of the business, the street address, and a phone number. There are various standards and formats available to choose from. You must carefully select the unit system, the default weight unit, and the time zone. Apart from all this, please select the right store currency. Depending on your country of operation, the store currency will differ.

Click on PowerSettings Payment providers

Configuring the payment method or the mode of payment is quite important. The first step is to set up your Shopify payments, then activate a third-party payment provider. You can also activate another method or alternative method of payment. Apart from this, don't forget to activate a manual payment method as well. Ensure that the payment authorization settings are secure and easy to remember.

Settings Shipping

As the name suggests, on this page in the settings menu, you can add or edit information about shipping origin, shipping rates, size and weight of packages, or even enable third-party fulfillment services. Shipping origin is the address used to calculate the overall shipping rate. Depending on the shipping zones and corresponding shipping rates, you can set specific shipping rates at the checkout. To calculate the shipping costs, don't forget to consider the size and weight of the packages that have to be shipped.

Settings Checkout

An important part of a well-functioning e-commerce website is the checkout page. On the checkout page, you can make changes to the customer account, customer contact, order processing, email marketing, checkout, language, and all the other policies associated with your e-commerce store. In customer accounts, you have the option to choose whether a customer must create an account before he can checkout or not. Customer contact essentially offers the choice of whether customers need to provide a specific phone number or their email address before checking out. It also gives you the option to choose any contact method the customers can use to receive shipping updates. Customer forms allow you to decide whether you want to collect any other additional information from the customer before they checkout or not.

In order processing, different details about the checkout process, such as the information on the checkout page, order fulfillment, billing address, and the shipping address, will be mentioned. For the sake of email marketing, you can offer a chance for your customers to sign up or subscribe to your email marketing campaigns. Don't forget to check the language for the checkout page. Apart from that, there are various policies, and you need to fill out the checkout page with details such as refund policy, terms of service, and the privacy policy.

Settings Notifications

This page essentially offers different notification settings like shipping notifications, customer notifications, and order notifications. The customer notifications are for any orders processed on your e-commerce stores, such as the information about invoices, order cancellations, order confirmations, order refunds, and abandoned shopping carts. The different shipping notifications include shipping update, fulfillment request, shipment or delivery, shipping confirmation, and shipping delivered. So, you have complete power to determine the kind of notifications you want or don't want to receive. When all the notification systems are in place, it helps ensure that your business is on the right track.

Settings Taxes

If you don't want to get into any legal trouble, then ensure that your store has all the necessary permissions and is paying all its taxes on time. Depending on the existing taxation policies in the country or the state the store is located in, the tax rates will differ.

Settings Sales

Managing your sales channels is quintessential for any e-commerce store owner. By using this option, you can easily manage or add sales channels to your existing e-commerce store. Sales channels help you to sell online through social networks, on mobile applications, or even in person.

Settings Files

Use this option for uploading videos, images, or any other documents. You can also manage all the files you upload using this setting.

Settings Billings

As the name suggests, this section essentially deals with all the billing associated with your Shopify store. Billing information provides information about all the invoices that are paid for using any of the chosen payment methods available on the website. You can also add a credit card to pay other invoices you have on this platform. To understand the overview of all the fees and payouts, such as the Shopify subscriptions, or even the shipping fees, don't forget to check the invoices and fee option.

Settings Account

On this page, you'll find all the details required to manage your Shopify account. It essentially provides an account overview, status of the account, and the Shopify plan you opted for. If you have any other staff accounts associated with your main Shopify account, then use the accounts and permissions options to manage all the other accounts. You can pause the store, close your Shopify store, or also hire an expert by using the store status option.

Step 4: Adding Products

Open the dashboard, select products, and then click on the option to add products. In this section, you can add new products to your e-commerce store so that you can sell them immediately. To get started, click on the "add product" button, and provide the required product title and any other additional information associated with the product. There are two methods you can use for uploading products. You can manually add products or bulk import them. To manually add products, you'll need to fill out details for every product like product description, title, image, category, variants, price, and so on. You can also bulk import all the products by importing them via a CSV (comma separated values) file.

If you don't have a product yet, you can use a duplicate product option. Once duplicated, you can make changes as and when you receive the new items. However, if you are interested in adding any variance to a specific product, then don't forget to click on the "add various" button.

Step 5: Assigning Products

Now, it is time to assign different products to various collections. To do this, click on the products option from the navigation menu, then go to collections, and then click on create collections option. Once you have created and added all the products, it is time to segregate them into particular collections. Different collections help to optimize the display of products in the menus available on your e-commerce store.

There are two ways in which you can add products to collections on your Shopify website. The first step is to add the products you want to different collections manually, and the second option is to add products automatically. If you opt for the automated route, then certain products will be automatically added to a specific collection whenever it meets certain preset criteria set by you.

Step 6: Applying Themes

Now, it is time to apply themes to your Shopify store. The first step is to open the dashboard, then visit the online store. Go to option setting and select themes. The Shopify theme store is quite simple to use, and you can get started with it right away. There are various free and paid-for themes available to choose from on Shopify. Every theme on Shopify comes with a preview. So, you can see the preview before you decide to apply it to your store. Once you opt for a specific theme, all you need to do is publish it on the Shopify store. You will learn more about the different themes available in the subsequent chapters.

Step 7: Customization

Customizing the navigation bar is also an important part of creating your Shopify store. The first step is to open the Shopify store, go to the sales channel section, and then click on the online store. In this option, opt for navigation, and from there on, click on the menu to add the links you want to add. In this space, you can add different navigational links a user can use to view your online store. You can add links to the "About Us" page, policy page, or even the "contact us" page. Think about all the different pages you wish to include in the Shopify website and then add the links for these in the navigation bar.

Step 8: Pages

You cannot have a website that doesn't have any pages on it. Once you have added all the links required, you then need to create the respective pages for them as well. To create pages, open the dashboard, and visit the online store option, and click on pages. There are different pages your website must include, such as the "about us," "contact information," FAQs, and policy pages. Ensure that these pages provide all the information a potential customer might need before purchasing from your e-commerce store.

Step 9: Blogs

You can also add blog posts and blog categories such as e-commerce news to your website. By adding some valuable content to the website, you are increasing the value it offers potential customers. When your customers know they stand to gain something from accessing your website, then their inclination to access your website will increase. It is also a great way to retain your customers while increasing loyalty.

Step 10: Customizing Themes

In the previous step, you were asked to select a theme for your Shopify store. After you select a theme, it is time to customize the theme to make your store look more attractive. During customization, you are required to upload the logo for your store, upload any slides of product images or deals to place a carousel feature on your homepage. You can also add related item functionality for all the product pages. In customization, you are required to choose the number of items that will show up on each line of the collection pages. Deciding the product placement and presentation is quite important because it creates the overall feel of the website.

Step 11: Domain

Shopify automatically displays a domain name for your online store. A domain name is the online address of your e-commerce store. Therefore, you need to have a domain name. The domain name should be attractive and easy to understand and remember. Shopify will automatically display a domain name for your e-commerce store free of charge. If you want, you can try this free option or purchase a customized domain name. If the domain name you opt for is already taken, then you are required to change the domain name.

Step 12: Store Preferences

To go through the store preferences, you need to go to the dashboard, click on the online store option, and then go to preferences from there. Ensure that you carefully go through all the different categories present in the store preferences option. The different categories, you need to pay attention to include Google analytics, title and Meta description, password protection, Facebook pixel, and checkout protection. The title and Meta description help ensure that your e-commerce store is optimized for search engines. By adding some Meta content to this, it allows the search engines to crawl and index your store, thereby increasing your online visibility. By enabling Google Analytics, you can keep track of all the visitors who visit the store. It also generates reports about different metrics and data you can use to come up with actionable insights for the sake of better marketing plans. As soon as your store is ready to go live, uncheck the password to make your store globally accessible. If you have or wish to launch a Facebook ad campaign, then enter the Facebook pixel ID to create online advertising campaigns. It helps track conversions, find new customers, and concentrate your marketing efforts. To protect your e-commerce store on Shopify from spam or abuse, complete the Google reCAPTCHA option at checkout.

Step 13: Paying for Shopify

Once you go through all these steps, it is time to select a specific Shopify plan to get started. There are five different plans available on Shopify, and they are as follows.

Shopify Lite

Shopify Lite costs $9 a month. If you are new to Shopify or want a trial run, then this is the cheapest option available. With Shopify Lite, you can showcase products on an existing website to different users on Facebook, and use Shopify to manage the sale of products, even at physical locations. If you have an existing website, then this option will come in handy.

Basic Shopify

Basic Shopify costs $ 29 per month, and it is the cheapest option available if you want to create your own e-commerce store on this platform. The various features it offers are unlimited file storage, supports two user accounts, allows you to sell unlimited products, offers customer support 24 hours a day, seven days a week, provides broad analysis, helps generate discount codes, and also supports the blog. Apart from this, it also supports manual order creation, offers complete access to e-commerce features, and helps recover abandoned carts.

Shopify

This plan from Shopify costs $79 per month, and it offers greater functionality benefits than the previous plans. It helps generate gift cards, recover abandoned carts at a better rate, provide advanced reports, and reduce the transaction fees. It also reduces the credit card fees payable on this platform. The option to generate gift cards will come in handy for any brand that desires to improve its recognition in the market. This plan from Shopify offers detailed summaries of customer and sales reports. It's ideal for anyone who has a high volume of online sales, sells products on gift cards can be issued, and requires detailed reports.

Advanced Shopify

This plan from Shopify costs $299 per month. With this plan, two functionalities are offered in addition to the ones offered by the previous plans. It not only offers advanced reports but also provides information about real-time shipping. This plan allows you to manage all the Shopify data easily while you create easily customizable reports. You can select from a variety of dimensions and metrics to create customized reports and save them for future reference. There are also a variety of filters you can apply to the data to obtain specific results that you wish to view.

Shopify Plus

This plan from Shopify costs $ 2000 per month. While this plan is the most expensive one available on Shopify. It is usually best suited to large companies instead of small and medium enterprises. This is a corporate solution that essentially offers all the features that have been mentioned up until now, and additional advanced functionalities like order fulfillment, security, and an application programming interface. Don't opt to do this unless you have an extremely high volume of sales, require advanced integration between the e-commerce store and other internal software, and have a massive budget.

Go through these different plans and opt for one that suits all your needs and requirements.

Step 14: Installing Apps

When it comes to Shopify, there are several thousands of apps to choose from. All these apps can be easily integrated with your e-commerce store. However, it is important to choose the right apps. The different apps you can use will help promote the online store, reward your customers, take care of shipping, track to revenue you on, and even manage inventory. Every function that you can think of that's necessary to run and maintain an e-commerce store can be taken care of by installing the app. Therefore, ensure that you carefully go through the list of different apps discussed in the subsequent chapters.

You merely need to follow the different steps given in this section to create a Shopify store within no time.

Chapter 3: Niche Marketing

A crucial part of financial success with an ecommerce career is discovering your niche market. A niche market sells a specific product or a small array of similar products directed at a specific group of potential customers who would be interested in buying from such a market. While you may think you might have more luck with having a large and diverse array of products available to your customers will be more likely to give you the upper hand, you really are better off deciding on the specific market you want to sell products in and focusing your efforts on that. This way you can identify yourself as a unique and valuable brand to your chosen market much more easily than if you were to become a generic estore that sells everything under the sun. Below is a little more information on niche marketing and how to master your chosen niche.

Choosing a Niche

Of course, the first step is deciding exactly which niche you want to specialize in. To do this, ask yourself:

- What are your interests, both personally and professionally? What products would you have fun selling or believe would be the best option economically?
- Ideally, you'll want to find a happy medium, depending on what your priorities are going into business.

Getting to Know Your Chosen Niche

If you're not already an expert in your chosen niche, become familiar with it before deciding to dedicate your business to selling products in such a market. Once you know what you're dealing with, let the world know how important your niche market products are.

Demonstrate their value by linking to your site in articles about products that you sell, or create your own articles explaining why your potential customers should value your products.

Reach out to sites that publish such articles and you'll be surprised how many would be happy to give a little free (or at least cheap) advertizing.

Planning Out Your Shopify Store

After you've decided what niche market you want to sell in and become familiar with your chosen market, it is still a good idea to plan out the details of how your store will run well in advance of creating the real thing. Ask yourself:

- What type of products are you going to sell? Are they going to be tangible or digital products? For example, if you decided you wanted to sell books you could either choose to sell printed books that are shipped to your customers or ebooks that can be downloaded immediately after payment. You could even do a little of both!

- How are you going to set up payments? Will you sell your products individually or will customers have access to them through subscription? For example, if you have a bookstore you could sell individual books and/or ebooks or decide to give online access to books through a subscription-based setup.

- What will be your store design? Will it make sense considering the products you're selling and niche market you're in? You will have the choice of Shopify's array of pre-made themes at your disposal. Or, if you wish, you can hire a web designer to create a unique theme for your site instead.
- How will you fulfill orders? Will you take advantage of Shopify's given shipping method, your own independent method, or will you use a dropshipper? If you decide to go with the given Shopify method, you will purchase and be sent shipping labels (postage included) for you to use to send packages to customers. Shopify users who go for the higher packages save more when using this method.
- What payment options will you have available to your customers? Will you use Shopify's given transaction tools or install your own method? Shopify provides several transaction options that can be added to your checkout page, such as Paypal.
- How will you get the products you are selling? Will you have the products in-house or involve a third party? Make sure that if you decide to purchase products that you then turn around and sell to other customers at a raised price that you'll be able to make a profit off of such a price customers would be willing to pay.

Chapter 4: Building Your Shopify Website

Initiating the setup of your Shopify store is an easy process. Compared to building a site from scratch, it is a piece of cake. That said, it takes time and requires practice before you can truly get your bearings, especially if you are not familiar with the intricacies of web design. Thankfully there are plenty of tutorials available and a manual you can view online to help you. Below are some basic guidelines to help you through the process of setting up your store.

1. Choosing a Package. There are multiple Shopify Packages to chose from, each designed for certain wants and needs for webstore creators from any walk of life. If you're only looking for the basics, you can go for a $9-$29 a month packages. (Packages that get you a store start at the $29 option.) If you'd like to get all the perks, you can go for the $179 a month package. Plus, there is a whole range of in-between package options to choose from if you're in a grey area. The higher the package you purchase, the more features you receive, such as reduced payment on processing fees, discounts on shipping labels, and extra features for your store.

2. Choosing a Theme. Shopify has a variety of theme options at your disposal -- over 100, and all of them free! If you don't mind paying a little more, you have the option of purchasing a premium theme, which cost between $80-$180. These themes come with higher quality features. You also have the freedom of foregoing Shopify's given theme options entirely and hiring a designer to create your own unique theme.

3. Adding Your Chosen Products. Once you've chosen what market niche and products you wish to focus on, you can start adding these products to your store. This is one of the most involved steps because there are a lot of intricate substeps to it that you might not have thought about beforehand. Not only are you posting a list products for your customers to see and hopefully purchase when your site goes live, but you are also organizing each product by style, size, color, and any other specifics that apply to them so your customer can easily find what they want. You have to incorporate images as well as text, plus descriptions of each product. Your products are the most crucial part of your website, so it makes sense that the bulk of your work focuses on them.

4. Adding Payment Options. One of the few drawbacks of doing business online is that paying for products is no longer as simple as cash, a check, or a card changing hands. Instead, you need to provide a list of payment options for your customers and integrate them into your website. On the Shopify platform you have multiple payment options, already integrated and ready to be used, to choose from, such as credit/debit cards and Paypal, plus a variety of less common choices. As mentioned before, you also have the choice of shipping your own products yourself with a postage label sent by Shopify or working with dropshippers who do the task for you.

Shopify Features, Add-ons & Tools

Shopify offers a plethora of extra features and tools to help you manage your business. Not only are there thousands of third-party tools you can use that are compatible with or easily work alongside Shopify, but the platform also offers some of its very own features and programs to make running your business that much more easily.

- Accounting Programs. Accounting is a crucial part of running a successful business. Shopify works alongside third-party accounting programs like Quickbooks, Freshbooks and Xero to help you with this sometimes daunting task. With these programs you can keep track of important financial information like your transaction history, taxes, and various expenses without the need of hiring a professional accountant.
- Inventory Management. Another key aspect of running your webstore is maintaining an inventory of your products. It is important to know you are stocked up enough for days of predictably high traffic, such as around upcoming holidays. You also need to be able to replace any missing or soon to be missing items before a customer orders that item from you.

With the help of Shopify's inventory management program you can easily see which products are more popular and which don't sell as quickly, and efficiently restock more or less often for each product as appropriate.

- Customer Service. Without your customers you would not even have a business. Therefore, you must have a reliable customer service. Whether it is about a complaint on their end or a notification about a shipped item sent from you, it is a good idea to set up auto-responder. This is especially useful once you've gained a larger traffic, as it is difficult, if not impossible, to manually respond to each and every email sent by a customer of a successful business or to let every single customer know when their package has sent. Even if it is an automated message your customer receives, it reassures them that you are listening and working on their problem. For those times where a customer does require human interaction, Shopify also offers tools like live chat so you or your staff can communicate with them directly.
- Social Media Management. In today's market, it is difficult to run a successful business without social media. Whether it is used for advertising, interacting with customers, keeping an eye on other businesses

in the market or all of the above, a Facebook page and any other social media equivalents is the way to go. It is recommended that you incorporate automated posts in your chosen social media outlet(s). While you can certainly interact with your customers via social media directly as well, automated posts are useful for scheduling content regularly or on specific dates without worrying to remember to do it yourself or needing to hire someone to do it for you. This also saves precious time that would have been spent fiddling with a blog or Facebook post to do something more productive, like responding to customer feedback or managing some other aspect of your business. There are a lot of options out there for social media management, many of them free and compatible with Shopify.

Chapter 5: Making Money on Shopify

Now come the most lucrative part and in fact, we can say the thing for which everyone works. Yes, that is money. Shopify is a wonderful platform to make money online. Here is a brief description of a few ways to earn cash with Shopify.

Establish your own store

It is certainly one of the most significant ways to make money with Shopify. The primary requirement is just to have something to sell! If you are not the owner of traditional bricks and mortar business, you can certainly take help of Drop Shipping. Here are some of the guidelines for drop shipping:

Affiliate Program

In case you don't have your own products for selling and you are not even interested in drop shipping , you can join the Shopify affiliate program with which you to earn up to $358 per customer using the option of customer referrals. In this, you have two options to choose from:

1. **Earn Residual Income in the form of Revenue Share as Your Monthly Income**

It's easy to earn commissions for all the Shopify customers referred by you on your website. The amount of commissions can go up to $35 per month.

2. **Earn Commission per Sale of a Client's subscription**

The website traffic influences your income to a large extent as the promotional contents available on the sites motivate the customers doing online searches to buy the products and thus boost your sales.

- Promote Shopify on Your Review Site

If you are not comfortable working on affiliate programs, you can make regular income just by running a review website on Shopify. It helps the customers in easily finding out the best and the most reliable products. In case your review website scores a high position in search engine rankings, it will certainly bring more Shopify sign ups to your site thereby helping to make more money. In order to gain such good income, you must have good traffic presence on your website which will help in enhancing the conversion rates.

- Show Creativity in Shopify Themes

If you are a person with a creative bent of mind, you can make customized themes to grab the attention of the customers.

- Create a Shopify App

It requires good programming skills. If you are good at it, you can design an App with the help of Shopify API and enhance the customer experience. Apps are a great way for your business to be mobile. You can not only have people looking at your products wherever they are, but they will also be able to quickly look and see if you've posted any updates.

The advantages of having an app are remarkable. You can not only make sure your customers are always up to date, but you can also make sure they know about all promotions and sales you'll be having. The advantages are great, if you have some way to make it.

Advantages of Using Shopify To Make Money

- Availability of Shopify packages at competitive rates.

- Availability a 14-day free trial demonstration.

- Free Ecommerce set up option.

- Easy to implement with GET STARTED option which provides an informative forum to get your site started in minutes. You just need to name your shop, add a short and catchy description to it specifying business contact details and the shop address.

- Even if you don't have products to sell, you can still make good amount using the Shopify affiliate program

How to Get more Sales on Social Media

Social media has been playing a pivotal role in boosting online sales nowadays. People make good use of the social media platform for making people aware about their products and grabbing their attention towards it.

For example, if you are interested in selling an iPhone case, the best way is to buy it from Ever buying for 4$ and then sell it for $10 keeping a margin of $6 at your Shopify store.

Not only this, but you can also create a discount code for 20% off and advertise it on Facebook, Twitter or Reddit for gaining the attention of more people towards it.

People love to buy gadgets using discount coupon codes and every day such sales are being done in huge numbers. Not only this, but you can also create Facebook stores and sell more products over there.

A Shopify store can be an exciting foray into digital retail, but you should also be mindful of potential obstacles and challenges along the way. Just like offline retail enterprises, an online store will test your patience, challenge your preconceived notions, and push you to your limits as far as knowledge and adaptability to changing trends and consumer preferences. This is especially true in the online commerce segment where your audience is constantly presented with a plethora of options.

The main thing to remember, as a Shopify storeowner, is to never lose sight of your primary goals in starting an e-commerce store. Whether your target is to have an additional source of income, or to eventually expand your online store into your main livelihood, long-term profitability and sustainability should be your focus rather than impulsive, hastily-decided, poorly-planned directions that can sidetrack you from financial freedom.

Chapter 6: Create Your Online Empire and Succeed in eCommerce Business with Shopify

Who wouldn't like to enjoy an online empire and do an impressive e-commerce business while sitting at home? To make your dream come true, let's first understand how to set up one's online store using Shopify.

Setting Up Your Online Store

Online store or online shopping is the latest buzz word you often get to hear. Here is an interesting offer from Shopify with a 14-day free trial that can be signed up from the main homepage. You can also click on the Free Trial button available on the menu bar. Provide your email, password, and create a store name.

The URL of the page contains your store name; however, if you wish to change it later, the page allows you to change. It is always better to create a simple name that reads like you.myshopify.com because choosing multiple words will show the link like your-business-name.myshopify.com. In case you don't want to be redirected to a URL from your domain like store.yourdomain.com to you.myshopify.com, then you must keep a store name/URL ready on hand. You will have to provide all your basic details such as name, address, and phone number while creating your account on Shopify. After these procedures, you will be taken to the admin dashboard to start creating your online store. Check out the 7 steps guide to ease the process.

1. Add your products

Start adding products to your store by manual addition or bulk upload from a CSV file or import from platforms like Magento and eBay. If you have digital products, then firstly, you need to install an app for digital product delivery, add your products using this app. The Shopify's online manual. Throws more light on the selling of digital products. If you have selling services that you are attempting to sell, then opt for an app like Product Options with which you can customize your service offerings. Shopify store allows you to have 100 variations for the products, which typically have options as for size, color, and finish. This site gives you the feasibility to add a product with a set of options, and there is no limit as such if it is a physical product. For example, you have 3 options for your e-book, i.e., just the e-book, the second is e-book along with supporting material, and a 3rd option, which is inclusive of everything plus access to a private member forum. The Shopify Documentation clearly tells you how to set up products.

2.   Customize your design

The next step is to add a custom design by choosing a theme. You can choose a theme from the Shopify theme store, which has various designs for free as well as paid. If you do not have any type of plan as such and simply chose some theme, you can always edit the theme by using the template editor or theme settings editor for modifying the coding. One common place where you would want to edit is the footer because that is the space you may choose for providing social links, payment methods, and various other details.

There will be some example themes that might be great to start out with. There are tons to choose from, but these ones are some of the best to look at off the bat.

3. Select Your Domain Name

The Shopify online manual encompasses all the information related to setting up of the custom domain name of your store. So, instead of being forced to choose a domain like you.myshopify.com, you can select from the options like store.yourdomain.com or yourdomain.com.

4. Set up Shipping and Tax Rates

You will be required to add taxes as well as additional shipping costs to your items and also notify Shopify about the same. Shopify would list the basic prices, but it depends on the product you sell, and you may need to customize more options.

5. Set up payments

This is a critical part of all the steps. Shopify Payments accept credit cards if you are in the USA, Canada, or the UK. This facility would not require any third-party payment gateways or merchant account. Shopify incorporates other payment processing services that include PayPal, Amazon Payments, and Google Wallet.

6. Settings

Your complete profile needs to be set up carefully. Most of these details get filled while you do it step-by-step. However, it doesn't ask for the information required for adding your Google Analytics code, store description, and store title in the profile section as all this information is required to be filled in the general settings.

7. Open Your Store and Prove it to the world

Once all the details are entered, and you are ready with your online store, you can make it public. Till such time, it will be password-protected, and you can also test the same to ensure if everything is functioning the way it is supposed to. Make sure that you check everything before the customer notices the loopholes.

Choosing Apps for Additional Functionality and Features

Shopify provides hundreds of free and premium apps which can be used to improvise your online store; they are categorized as:

Accounting — Link your Shopify store to any of the popular accounting solutions such as QuickBooks, Fresh Books, and Xero.

Customer Service — It always helps both the customer and the seller if you add contact forms, live chat, feedback, and other features for customer support.

Inventory — Inventory management systems, if integrated with your online store, will help in the process simplification.

Marketing — This category helps you include your email, search, and social media marketing into your online store.

Reporting — You can check for additional analytics related to your online business with the usage of these apps. It will help you in measuring conversion rates, sales data, as well as customer behavior.

Sales — This category helps you in increasing sales with the help of product reviews, customer loyalty programs, upsells, and recommendations given by others.

Shipping — Create your product shipment process easier and simpler with apps that help in managing the order fulfillment process and link you with your preferred shipping service.

Social Media — This is one category not to be missed on. Keep yourself connected with the customers and engage them on social media platforms using these apps.

Tools — You will find tools that would help you in handling all the features required for running an online store successfully. The best part and the most convenient thing for the users is that it also offers setting up bulk redirects, fighting fraud, language translators, as well as RSS feeds.

Unsure of where and how to start your online store, then you may have to reconfigure your SEO settings for your product pages and, in addition to that, add email marketing support so that the customers can be added to your email list. These email marketing services often guide you on how to connect your Shopify store to their system.

Social Selling

This has become a totally new concept of selling and widely used these days. If you are one person who wants to sell products on your blog, then here it is. Shopify provides plugins and widgets for WordPress, Drupal, and Joomla users by which you can show products in your posts, pages, and sidebar. If you are creating content based on customer's interest, this will increase traffic to your domain. Another interesting way to keep your customers in the loop and engaged is to create a Facebook page and also post interesting stuff. Shopify offers various Facebook integrations that would allow you to turn your Facebook page into an e-commerce store.

What About Affiliates?

Shopify offers various apps that allow you to create your own affiliate program to keep track of referrals made by customers and supporters. You can do this if you would not mind sharing your profits with others. This will also create some publicity.

Where You Can Go to Learn More

If you are someone with zeal to learn about eCommerce and succeed in marketing your online store, then there is no stopping. You can simply find reading material like e-books, guides, tutorials, and videos to help you learn more at Ecommerce University. You could also check Shopify Wiki, where you can go through everything you are required to know about while using Shopify and the design/development of your store. Shopify also has a support section in which you can find over 200 troubleshooting articles. Just in case, if you happen to come across some new or weird issue, you even have forums to look for support. Forums often have thousands of topics related to e-commerce.

Where You Can Get Help

This is the last resort wherein if you fail to help yourself with the troubleshooting guides. You can always seek expert help from the Shopify Experts. This area provides help with the store setup, designers, developers, marketers, and photographers who can indeed make your e-commerce store into a successful business.

Chapter 7: Getting the Right Keyword Shopify

We are going to talk about keyword research and how it applies to improving your store's visibility in search engines and how to target paid advertisements. This market research, however, will lay the groundwork for those tasks. Additionally, you'll be able to learn about your market simply by understanding the search habits of your prospective customers.

The first thing you can do is simply run a quick Google search for the types of products you want to sell and see what comes up. Google's search bar will also show you some similar search terms along the way, and it is often wise to take the time to look these over as well. Largely, this is going to show you what type of content people are seeing when they search for the same thing. Once again, it gives you a chance to size up the competition, and it also helps give some ideas about what you can do to improve upon what's already available to everyone.

Taking this much further, I want you write down a list of keywords and phrases that apply to the type of products you want to sell, common topics surrounding your market, and specific product names. I would type this list up so you can easily copy and paste later.

Next, it's time to use these words by taking advantage of Google's Keyword Planner. This tool is designed to help you create ads and appropriate bids for these ads on Google Adwords, the advertisement service that Google offers and uses on its own search results. You can get enough information without opening any ad campaigns to make this worth your while.

In Google's Keyword Planner, type in the keyword you have in mind, and it will pull up quite a bit of information. This software offers suggestions for related keywords, information on how often the keywords have been searched within a month, and a generalized idea of how much people are paying to place ads that show up when these keywords are typed into a search bar or are related to the page they're displayed on.

This data is valuable for many reasons. It is not going to show you a direct number of sales or how much money people are spending on any particular product or category of products, but it will help you understand if a market or product is trending, if people are actively seeking information or products by using these keywords, and just how competitive it is. While a high competition rate through the Keyword Planner doesn't mean you won't sell a certain product or can't break into a certain niche, it does mean that people will have a harder time finding this product on your ecommerce store through Google.

It is wise to write down those keywords and key phrases that have low competition and a moderate to large number of searches per month. If possible, it is ideal to incorporate these keywords and key phrases into your product titles and descriptions in an organic manner. We'll discuss this more later, but write these down while you're at it, and keep them somewhere you'll remember to find them later.

If you're unsure of the direction you aim to go with your ecommerce business, keyword research may be the best starting off point. If you can find a niche with large amounts of searches but low amounts of competition, that suggests that the competition isn't spending a lot of money on advertising these products, which makes it easier for you should you go that route. Additionally, it generally suggests that you will have the possibility of becoming one of the first-page results when people type in this phrase or word. Many entrepreneurs have used Keyword Planner and similar tools to pinpoint untapped niches in the past, and despite the growth of ecommerce over the last ten years, it is still possible to find a market that hasn't been completely saturated.

Another great thing about this type of keyword research is that it can help you name your shop, your domain name, and products with keywords that work well within search engines.

Search Engine Optimization (SEO) is an ever-evolving study and implementation of how to best make your website visible on search engines, especially Google. It is a highly involved topic, but a few key points can be applied to all your content, whether that's your blogs, product descriptions, video descriptions on YouTube, social media posts, or any other faucet of your online presence. Knowing the basics will help you avoid common blunders that hurt your rankings. While the best approach to SEO is working with a professional, these tips will at least help you get started.

- **Content is King**

Above all suggestions with SEO, the most important thing is that you are producing QUALITY content that is well written, proofread, and 100% original. Anything that isn't high quality is going to hurt you one way or another. Quality content is what builds trust in your name, and that high reputation will eventually translate to your positioning within search engines.

If you're not a great novelist, it may be imperative to have someone edit/proofread your work. If you know someone that will help, then by all means ask for their help. Offer to pay them back with your services, products, or even just money. If you don't know anyone, hiring a decent freelancer from sites like Upwork is suggested.

To ensure your original content isn't flagged a plagiarism, use CopyScape (or other plagiarism checkers), and scan your content 500 words at a time. This will let you know if there's anywhere else on the internet where the words you've written already exist verbatim. Avoid reusing manufacturer descriptions and pictures for this reason.

Again, no amount of SEO work matters if you don't produce excellent content. This is the most important thing you can do.

- **Implement Keywords**

Using that method, you should be able to create a relatively long list of keywords and order them from most likely to succeed to least important. As a rule of thumb, a high search count with a low competition is helpful.

I've suggested the implementation of keywords in many instances throughout the product description, blog, etc. As a rule of thumb, a keyword should not be utilized more than once per 100-200 words. Stacking a keyword too many times on a single page can cause Google's algorithm to flag your site as spam.

Never implement keywords in a way that doesn't work organically. As your content must be quality, shoving in a keyword awkwardly just hurts your chances of sales even if it does happen to increase your rankings on Google.

Use your keywords in meta data fields, titles, your domain name if possible, and basically every spot you can. Even if you can only fit it in once, it is better to have it than not to have it.

You can write blog posts around your key words. Not only is this a good way to give yourself something to write about, but it ensures that you're using keywords in an organic and intelligent manner. Anyone can stack a page with keywords, but only great writers and smart SEO strategists can write a brilliant article around any given keyword.

- **Images and Video**

Images and video, especially when they're original content, will greatly help with your search engine visibility. Not only does this help integrate your site into the Image and Video search features on Google, but it also gives you another chance to incorporate keywords within the alt-text and the video's description.

Chapter 8: Steps in Planning your Pricing Strategy

How much should you sell your product for?

The price is a characteristic of your product. It's part of its branding and of its market positioning—its place in the market compared to other similar offers (competitors).

Pricing is therefore an important element to consider when you build your business, not only as a mean of generating revenues, but also as an element that impacts how your product will be perceived by potential consumers.

Pricing is often an element of discomfort among new entrepreneurs. Likely caused by a lack of experience and thus confidence, putting a price on a new product or service can make many new business owners nervous.

Many entrepreneurs don't know how much to charge and aren't sure of the value of the new product. They might also fear the market's reaction. Will they think the price is too high? What if they leave a comment on the web saying, "It certainly wasn't worth the cost!"?

However, remember the definition of a business: getting remunerated for the value you bring to a market. There shouldn't be any shame in getting paid for providing value.

Pricing Is (First) a Psychological Thing

If you keep your price low because of a lack of confidence in your own product, it will show. The price of a product is often associated with its (perceived) quality. If you think that by offering your product at a very low price, you'll avoid potential complaints and will navigate in a safer zone, don't be so sure.

Before we get into more detail, I would like to share a little story.

A short time ago, I was part of a mastermind group of web entrepreneurs and bloggers. At the first meeting, we all introduced ourselves. One member was a life coach. He introduced himself and explained what he was doing, with obvious confidence:

"Come to see me once, and you will feel aligned and get the ability to be laser-focused on what you are meant to achieve in life. Just one session with me will change your life." Wow. Even I wanted to book an appointment with him right away. His speech was very convincing. Then, we asked him how much he was charging per session. I expected $1,000. He could have said $1,500, and it would have seemed justified. However, he said $250, for one hour of his time. What do you think happened in my mind? Did I think "What a bargain!"?

Well, not exactly. It made me doubt his promise and the result he was selling. In just a one-hour session with him, my life would be changed, for only $250. Something felt wrong about that. That "something" was the cost of his service. It was simply too low, and that low price diminished the perceived quality of his offer.

Do you see how pricing is primarily a psychological thing?

Does this mean it's better to sell your offerings at a higher price just to increase the perceived value? Well, no... but the displayed price should be in accordance with the benefit you are promising.

Pricing is also often related to status. Some people will always buy the most expensive watches and shoes because they want their "social status" to show in their clothing and accessories.

Your chosen positioning strategy in the market—your product compared to your competitors'—should also have an influence when determining the price, as it's one element that consumers will use to evaluate your offer.

Whatever price you are willing to let your product sell for, there should be a good reason to back it up. A lower price isn't necessarily a bad thing, if you justify it. The same is true for a higher price.

How to Define the Price of Your Product

What is the Purpose of Your Product?

The first question to answer is: "Why are you offering this product in the first place?"

Is it to:

- Gain credibility? (Often the case in publishing a book or creating a blog)

- Get more email subscribers to your website?

- Generate revenue?

Why does the purpose of your product matter? If you hope to collect leads (email subscribers), then you have a reason to give your product away or at a lower price, since the emails alone have a high value. In this case, a low price won't diminish your product's perceived value. It will be justified, and even advantageous, since you want to get as many quality visitors to subscribe to your list as possible.

If you wish to gain credibility, then money isn't the main goal, either. You shouldn't settle for a very low or very high price, but more for something in the middle. However, if you want to generate revenue, then yes, you should aim for a higher price.

What's the Paying Capacity of Your Target Market?

If you've done some research into your avatar's (ideal customer's) profile, you should have an idea about its income, its discretionary budget, and its willingness to pay for the type of product you are offering.

What *could* your audience pay for your product?

If your target market is single parents on benefits or college students, and you're selling a giant home cinema screen, there's a good chance that this market, even if interested in your offer, won't have the ability to pay for it.

Ask yourself: "Can they pay?"

This is an important aspect to consider when deciding on a niche. Ideally, you want to serve a market that has discretionary income to spend on non-essential goods.

What is the Market's Reference Price?

What's the price for similar options offered in the market? At what price are your competitors selling comparable products? That should also be a good indicator. Look at your competitors' product characteristics and related pricing. Compare the characteristics of their offer versus yours. Then, think of the position in the market that you would like to occupy. Are you a low-cost, average, or high-end option?

Cover Your Costs

What is your fixed cost, or the cost you pay independently of how many items you create? What are your variable costs, or the cost per product created?

For example, if you write a book, your fixed cost will include the production of your book, including the writing time, the cover illustration, the editing, and proofreading.

The variable cost will include the printing and distribution fees per book.

Unless you've decided to give your product away for free, you'll want to cover both your fixed and variable costs. If the purpose of creating your product is to generate revenue, then you may want to sell it for at least three times its variable cost of production. On the other hand, if the purpose is to generate leads (subscribers), then you might not need to cover your costs, since it will be considered more as an investment.

What's the Perceived Value of the Benefit Your Customers Will Gain After Consuming Your Product?

How beneficial is the result provided by your offer to your target market? What's the perceived value of that benefit?

For example, how much would a person who wants to lose ten pounds to look great before the summer be willing to pay for a weight loss program? What about a woman who wants to fit into her wedding dress? Or a man who needs to lower his cholesterol to avoid imminent health problems?

Your target market will be sensitive to price depending on the importance of overcoming the "pain" as well as its urgency.

Also, what will it take for your customers to overcome the "pain"? If you're offering a weight loss program that guarantees good results within two months by following an exercise and healthy cooking plan, how much would the average person who wants to lose weight quickly be ready to pay? How much would that same person be willing to pay for a simple, natural pill that guarantees the same results? Probably more than the exercise plan, as the effort required for achieving the result is smaller.

The benefits to be gained by using the product, and the effort required, should be considered when deciding on the product's price.

The Mattress Method

Marie Forleo, business coach and entrepreneur, has a great way of explaining the perceived value of a product: The Mattress Method. Can you translate the value of your product into real-life currency, like time, money, love, and health?

She gives an example of the day she went shopping for a new mattress. The mattress she was looking at was more expensive than other types offered on the market, but the salesman reminded her that:

- You spend one-third of your time in bed

- Good sleep improves your productivity, health, and good looks

Essentially, the salesman told her that good sleep contributed in making her richer, healthier, and prettier. These are the tangible benefits of the product in real-life currency. What is the perceived value of the benefits your customers will gain after purchasing your product?

Your Portfolio of Products

You should offer multiple levels of products or services.

For example, if you have an eBook selling for $19, an online course at $79, and a one-hour consultation at $250, you have a portfolio of three products. Offering multiple levels of products gives people a price reference point.

In the example above, if you only sell an eBook and an online course, the online course may be perceived by consumers as too expensive, but when you add a pricier item—the $250 consultation—to the portfolio, it makes the middle offer seem more affordable. It's psychological. Most people will opt for the middle option.

Another reason to consider a product portfolio might surprise you: some people will only want the high-end option. If you don't offer a high-end option or a more expensive product, they will buy one elsewhere.

In the book 80/20 Sales and Marketing, Perry Marshall explains that there will always be people willing to buy a very expensive offer. He gives the example of Starbucks. Starbucks sells cups of regular filter coffee for $2.50. You can also buy a complete breakfast for about $12, including a soy latte, biscotti, and a fruit salad. But have you noticed the espresso machine also available for sale? Of course, not many customers will buy the $400 espresso machine, but a few will. If Starbucks didn't offer an espresso machine, the customer who wanted to buy one would get it from somewhere else. Starbucks would lose a sale for not offering the product.

Do you have a high-end product to offer? If not, can you create one? Not only will offering one make your other, lower cost products look more affordable to your customers' eyes, but not offering one will most likely cause you to lose potential sales.

The bottom line is to offer multiple levels of products or services. It helps people to make a purchase decision when they can compare products and prices.

Discounts Are Dangerous

As a rule, it's better to avoid offering discounts.

Discounted rates are addictive. When people see your product offered at a discount, they'll have a harder time buying it at the regular price later. They may expect further discounts and wait for one before buying.

Plus, discounting can evoke confusion towards the perceived quality of the product you are offering. If it's sold for less, does that mean it's worth less than what it was offered for?

The question is: What should you do instead?

A better approach is to add extra value for a limited time. In the context of a launch, this may include adding another item to the original offer as a bonus.

For example, if you're selling an online course on outdoor photography, you could offer a free eBook on how to take great sunrise and sunset shots to the first 10 buyers.

If your product is a book, you could offer the audio version at no extra fee, for a limited number of copies sold or for a limited time.

It's a bargain for your audience without diminishing the perceived value of your main product or accustoming consumers to discounted prices. Note that the bonus item should be relevant to the main product and, ideally, should complement it.

If You Really Want to Offer a Discount

In this case, be sure to justify the discount. Give a reason for why you are offering it.

Is it for clearance? Is it your organization's 10th anniversary, so you'll happily give away a discount to celebrate? Or are you giving a special discounted offer to your most loyal customers to thank them?

Whatever the reason, mention it. Let people know that this is for a special occasion to make sure they won't expect frequent discounts in the future.

All-inclusive resorts in regions near the tropics offer discounted rates during the northern hemisphere summer, because fewer people are buying their vacation products during that period. That's justified. They have a reason to lower the price, as the low season means less occupancy. These resorts could do even better—they could upgrade their regular offer. Instead of discounting the price of a room, they could offer dining vouchers or free excursions during the low season.

Don't Worry About People Complaining About Your Product's Price

RamitSethi, author of I Will Teach You To Be Rich, has been asked many times to talk about pricing on different podcasts and live shows, such as The Smart Passive Income or Chase Jarvis Live.

He admitted to having had trouble charging for his products at the beginning. He feared his audience's reaction, even if his first product was a five-dollar eBook! And yes, some members of his audience did complain.

"How dare you charge us for your content?!"

Ramit had been delivering valuable information, for free, for about two years before selling his $5 eBook.

Well, what does this teach us? It tells us that there will always be those who complain!

Fortunately, these complainers usually only constitute a very small percentage of an audience, and they aren't part of an audience that you want to serve. They don't represent your ideal customer. Ramit's audience members who complained about the $5 eBook, even after they had happily consumed two years of valuable free content, weren't worthy of his attention.

The bottom line is that there will always be unhappy people, and that's okay. Live with it, and stop fearing putting a price on your product.

That said, if the complaints you're getting with regards to your product's price are generalized, maybe you did do something wrong. In that case, listen to the constructive negative feedback, and, if possible, modify your price accordingly.

What to Remember About Pricing?

1. Pricing is part of branding and positioning.

2. Pricing is very psychological:

3. It's often associated with quality.

4. It can also be related to status.

5. To determine your product's price, there are some elements to consider:

6. The purpose of your product

7. The paying capacity of your target market (niche)

8. The market's reference price (other similar options offered on the market)

9. The perceived value of the solution or benefit your product provides

10.   It's better to offer multiple levels of products in order to have a portfolio of products of different value and at different prices.

11.   Instead of discounting your product, offer bonus items for a limited number of purchases or for a limited time to add extra value. This way, it won't diminish the perceived value of the original offer, and it will avoid accustoming your customers to discounted rates.

Chapter 9: Comparing Shopify to Other Ecommerce Platforms

If you are reading this book, it is clear you are considering Shopify as the platform for your ecommerce website. Not only is this book meant to teach you all about how to run a successful estore business, but it is also meant to teach you about the benefits of Shopify over other Ecommerce Platforms. To give you a balanced and fair comparison, we will discuss a handful of the top platforms around, as well as each of their advantages and disadvantages compared to Shopify.

What Exactly is an Ecommerce Platform?

An ecommerce platform is a software program that provides a template for building an ecommerce website. It skips the majority of painstaking hassle that comes with building a site from scratch, like coding and dealing with the complex aspects of designing such a website. Your responsibility is simply to customize everything to your liking by choosing from a variety of designs already pre-made and bug-free.

Stacking Shopify Against Other Ecommerce Platforms

Shopify is easily the most widely used ecommerce platform out there, even among hundreds, even thousands, of other competitive platforms. That said, that does not necessarily mean it is the best. Below we'll pit Shopify against three other platforms -- Magento, BigCommerce and Volusion -- all of which are joined by Shopify in the top five platforms in the industry. We will focus on eight main features: Pricing, design customization, features, security, marketing, reports, add-ons and support, and by the end you will hopefully have adopted an informed and unbiased opinion on which is the best platform.

Pricing. When it comes to cost, Magento is the cheapest because it is free unless you choose to purchase the Enterprise Edition, which is fairly costly. BigCommerce is the most expensive, as it offers four tiers of packages, much like Shopify does, but the monthly cost for each is about twice as much as Shopify's. Finally, Volusion's prices are quite similar to Shopify's.

Design Customization. For each platform, custom designs are available from a variety of theme options. Some of these theme options are free and some cost money. BigCommerce doesn't charge for any of its themes, but the quality of them is pretty low. Volusion, once again, is comparable to Shopify in theme cost and quality -- it offers a couple dozen themes for free and also a larger selection of premium ones with quality similar to Shopify's. Magento also has a selection of free themes but the quality ones cost money and are pricey. Shopify and Volusion maintain the best balance between price and quality.

Frontend Features. Each of these platforms are very similar when it comes to features on the frontend. The one platform from the group that might be a little lacking is BigCommerce because it lacks organization. However, it does make up for it by offering more features than any of the other three platforms, including Shopify.

Backend Features. Unlike with frontend features, there's nothing lacking from BigCommerce when it comes to the backend. This platform offers plenty of customization features on a clean interface to let you make the store look and feel like your own. Shopify comes in as a close second, also with an easy-to-use interface. Volusion and Magento have backends that are harder to wrap your head around and take a bit of time to get used to.

Security. This is the category where Shopify steps up as the superior platform. Shopify's hosting is top notch and it has a Content Delivery Network (CDN) and is PCI compliant. BigCommerce comes in second place, as it is also a secure host but does not have a CDN. Volusion does provide hosting, a CDN and PCI compliance but you have to buy the encryption that Shopify offers for free. With Magento you'd need to get outside hosting, which is more money out of pocket, but since the basic edition of the platform doesn't cost anything it kind of balances it out.

- Marketing. Marketing does not just mean advertisement, but includes social media, SEO, and other aspects. Once again, BigCommerce delivers the best quality as the platform's great customization abilities extends to SEO customization. Magento is second best, with everything you need for SEO already programmed in and ready for use. Shopify only offers basic SEO features and Volusion offers even less. Each platform seems to be on equal footing as far as social media integration is concerned, excluding Magento, which doesn't offer it. Volusion and Magento offer a newsletter feature while Shopify and BigCommerce offer the ability to add a third-party integration.

- Promotions. Each platform offers about the same types of promotions. They also each offer a marketing tool that helps you bring in more traffic.

- Reports. Again, each platform is pretty much on the same footing for this category.

- Add-ons. All four platforms offer add-ons that give you the opportunity to use more features than you originally had. Each platform has an app store you can look through and install from. It is hard to pick the best platform for this category because apps are always changing and it's difficult to measure them up against each other if they never stay the same.

- Support. With Shopify, you are guaranteed unlimited support, 24/7, regardless of your chosen package. BigCommerce offers 24 hour support on weekdays and select hours on weekends, as well as an education center for estore builders. Volusion offers support via phone, live chat and email 24/7, while Magento lacks proper support unless you purchase the pricey package upgrade. Short of doing that, you can visit the site forums for help and guidance.

Chapter 10: Sourcing for Suppliers

Before you set out to look for suppliers, we value your business and would not want you to get cheated. It is essential to distinguish between valid wholesalers and retailers posing as such. We already differentiated in defining the two and the terminologies, feel free at to scroll back up to remind yourself of the differences. Note that there are retailers that claim to be wholesaler but are not. Legitimate wholesalers buy directly from manufacturers and offer much lower prices than retailers.

Here Is How You Identify Fake Wholesalers:

Unfortunately, real wholesalers very rarely invest in marketing and are usually much concealed. This means that by the time you find a legitimate wholesaler, chances are you will come across very many fake ones. You also should be wary of swindling middlemen, but fortunately, you have us and we have you.

- They will ask for ongoing fees: Have you ever been asked to pay an application fee to be accepted for a certain job? If yes, then you probably realized that you got conned. This is the same with such 'wholesalers. They will ask you to pay a monthly fee to grant you the privilege of working with them. Two words, RED FLAG! Real suppliers will never ask you to pay ongoing fees.

However, distinguish between suppliers and their directories. We shall look at directories shortly, but they are likely to ask you to pay a certain fee, however, theirs would be legitimate and be reasonable.

- Open to the public: Wholesalers do not sell to the public, and if this wholesaler does, they are simply a falsely poised retailer cheating the public with their hyperinflated prices. However, you need to be registered as a legitimate business and have a wholesale account. You also need to have been approved before you make your first purchase.

Here are some fees you will incur:

➢ Per Order: Many and most drop shippers will charge you a fee for every order you make. This will probably range somewhere between two and five dollars. It is all a matter of complexity and the size of the products that are being drop shipped. Note that you are not being conned, this is a standard of operation in this industry.

➢ Minimum order: Wholesalers will always have a minimum purchase number. This is done to ensure that they get rid of window shoppers who are a nuisance and people with small orders that won't translate to important business.

➢ If you are drop shipping, then this will come with its own complications. What would you if a supplier has a minimum purchase of around six hundred dollars and your business' average order is two hundred dollars? In such a situation, your best option would be to prepay the supplier the six hundred dollars. This allows you to build credit with them.

Identifying Suppliers

Having the knowledge to know identify who's real and who's not, it's time to find you some suppliers. Live everything in life, there are several strategies you could employ to find a supplier that is in line with your goals. We listed the methods below basing them in the order of effectiveness and preference.

- *Contact Them:* We highlighted somewhere above in this pile of words that phone calls work miracles. Call the manufacturer and find out what they have to offer by simply asking for a list of their products. Also, find out whether they drop ship or not. This is a basic.

- *Google:* Google is indeed your friend. This is obvious, why didn't we start with this? Well, because, there are several things you need to keep in mind,

- *Carry out an extensive search:* Let us again revisit and old point of wholesalers being terrible at marketing, but no offense to them. This means that your top searches will probably not what you are looking for. But look at this a challenge, when is the last time you clicked 'next page' on a Google search? Now you have a reason to.

- *Website aesthetics could be misleading:* While how appealing a website looks like could be a good indicator for how serious a business is, this may not entirely apply to suppliers, especially wholesalers. Do not skim through a website and jump on to the next because that one did not look good.

- *Use as many modifiers as possible:* I'm sure you've heard enough times already, so here it is again. Wholesalers do not invest in marketing and will not do any Search Engine Optimization. Try using as many words that will distinctively bring up exact results for what you are looking for, words such as a distributor, warehouse, bulk, and supplier.

- *The competition is your friend:* Wait, what? Yes, your completion could help you identify a supplier. How do you ask? Simple. Place a small order with a competitor who is drop shipping. Once you receive your package, simply Google the returns address that is on the package. And bingo, you have identified who the original shipper of the package is. Contact them next.

- *Trade Shows:* Trade shows offer one major advantage, centralization. Attending a trade show allows you to interact with potential suppliers all in one single spot. This only works, however, once you have already identified a niche market and know what product you want to deal with.

- *Directories:* Here we are! We said that you should not confuse suppliers and their directories. So, what are directories anyway? A directory is a database of suppliers, simple. They are usually sorted in accordance to market, niche, and items. Now comes the question, why should you pay for supplier directories? This is because most of the companies that run supplier directories are for-profit, thus will charge you to let you access you their database. However, to prevent monthly subscription and other expenses by supplier directories, ensure that you conduct your research and know from the get-go what specifically you are looking for. Identify your market niche and products then it will require a bit of searching to find what is it you are looking for.

Here are some supplier directories that offer impeccable services; Doba, Wholesale Central, Worldwide Brands and SaleHoo.

Before You Contact Them

Now that we've taken through criteria of sorts for identifying potential supplier and are ready to contact them, there are a few things that need to be in check before you do so.

- Is your business legal? Is your business legal? As we have constantly mentioned, almost all wholesalers will require you to certify that your business is legal. They also tend to only reveal their pricing to legally registered businesses. If you just need basic information then that you shall get without any documentation, but to be fully incorporated in the system and get the inside scoop, your business should be fully legitimate.

- Understand your and the general reality: You need to know that supplier will not go any extra mile, not even an inch to help you out. Similarly, everyone else who contacts them makes promises and tells them how great their plans are. They've heard it before; they've heard it all. All suppliers need is credibility. Be definitive in your statements and answers, use terms like 'we have', 'we are'. Mention things that carry some weight and remember to mention any professional experience you have. Avoid using phrases like 'I think." Do not ask for favors too soon and be as convincing as you possibly can.

- The phone is your friend: The idea of making phone calls especially to people who are deemed as our superiors is always frightening. But phone calls are a very efficient way of getting things done. Phone calls are not as scary as you think. Suppliers are also accustomed to receiving phone calls thus you will be attended to.

Attributes of Good Suppliers

- Expert Staff: One good indication of a credible supplier is its staff. Good suppliers will have representatives who understand the industry quite well. You can tell this from how they answer questions.

- Committed support: Essentially, suppliers are supposed to allocate you're your own sales representative for a streamlined flow of business. The sales rep is supposed to take care, handle and fulfill your needs. It is very frustrating to have to call suppliers and nag them to fix a certain issue.

Therefore, the sales rep acts as the bridge between the two entities.

- Technology: As time goes by, the key to remaining successful in the industry is adaptability. This is an easy way to know what kind of supplier you are dealing with. If they are invested in technology, then they will be a pleasure to work with. They will offer you real time feeds on inventory, shipping, catalogs, and the like. Imagine a supplier that still handles all that manually.

- Accepts orders through email: This may sound minor and negligible, but some suppliers do not accept orders via email. Pause for a minute and think about having to place every single order via phone and whether that system sounds effective to you.

- Location: In this business of drop shipping, location is one of those factors that carry a lot of weight. Find a supplier that is in the middle of the country, especially if you live in a big country such as the United States or Canada. Why? This is because, if a supplier is located at one end of the country, it will take too long to get orders to the other end fulfilled. The ideal fulfillment period is two to three days, keep that in mind.

- Efficiency and organization: This are difficult to measure and calculate. How do you know whether someone you have never worked with is organized and efficient? Simple, work with them. How? Place an order or two and be the judge. This will tell you a lot about a drop shipping supplier.

How to Pay Suppliers:

There are two ways in which suppliers accept payments:

Credit cards: Most suppliers will require you to pay using a credit card as you're starting out. As your business grows and flourishes, credit cards are still the best option for payments because they can rack up a lot of reward points.

Net terms: Net terms means that you are provided with several days to pay for items you purchased. For instance, when you are on 'net 40' terms, this means that you have forty days, which are counted from the date of purchase to pay for the goods, either by check or bank.

Chapter 11: Marketing your Shopify Store

The idea of any Shopify store is to increase the traffic, and overall rate of conversions. Even if you know the goal you are going after, it can become a little tricky to choose the ideal marketing tactics to attain the goals. As an e-commerce store, you cannot increase your sales unless the traffic on your website is high. It is not just the traffic that matters, but the rate of conversion matters too. In this section, let us look at some effective marketing tactics you can use to market your Shopify store online effectively. Don't be in a rush, and don't try to implement all the ideas at once. Instead, pace yourself and try implementing them one at a time. By doing this, you can effectively figure out the strategies that are and aren't effective for your business.

Before we get started with learning about marketing the Shopify store, it is important to understand what e-commerce marketing means. E-commerce marketing is a simple practice of using various promotional methods to drive traffic to a specific online store, converting the said traffic into paying customers, and retaining the customers while increasing the customer base. An ideal e-commerce strategy consists of various marketing tactics that help build brand awareness, improve customer loyalty and customer retention, and ultimately lead to an increase in the overall sales of a business. You can use the tactics discussed in this section to promote your online store or increase the sales of a specific product.

Reducing Abandoned Carts

Try to understand that your business is potentially losing money whenever a user or a visitor abandons his cart without making a purchase. Plenty of visitors can easily add items to their carts, but they tend to abandon them for various reasons before completing the checkout process. Try to address as many of the hesitations as shoppers might have. The simplest way to reduce the rate of abandoned carts is by gently reminding the visitors about their abandoned carts. Perhaps you can persuade them by offering free shipping or even a discount.

A simple yet effective e-commerce marketing idea to reduce the frequency of abandoned carts is by using email recovery campaigns. Go through the different tips discussed in the previous chapter to build an email list. Once your email list is in place, you can email them whenever you notice that the users in your list didn't complete a purchase or have abandoned their carts on your website. For instance, the email you can send such users could be along the lines of, "Did you forget something? ___ are still waiting for you in the cart!" Whatever email responses designed need to be quite enticing and should remind those juice or why he was purchasing the products in the first place.

Upselling

Upselling is an incredible tactic that has been used by marketers since forever. Upselling merely means increasing the cart value or the order value. You might have probably heard some variation of a sentence that essentially means, "Would you like to increase your cart value?" Instead of working on acquiring new customers, upselling can be quite profitable too. At times, customers are not aware of all the premium products available, or they probably need more guidance to understand how an upgraded package is better suited for their needs. For instance, if you are selling handmade leather items, then to upsell the items, you can add leather polish, brush, or even wax to increase the cart value. You can also come up with enticing combos to tempt the users to increase their overall cart value. By doing this, if a buyer who would have spent $ 20 on one purchase can end up spending $ 30 on a purchase. It might not sound like much in easily, but over a period, the amount earned from up selling will certainly add up.

There are two important considerations while you use upselling to increase the sales of your business. Ensure that the product you are upselling is directly related to or is complimentary with the original product. The second point is to be sensitive to the anticipated price range of your target audience. The product must not only fit your customer's original needs, but it needs to be within the price range that your target audience might not want to exceed.

Using Instagram

Gone are the days when social media was restricted to just Facebook. One of the most powerful and frequently used social media platforms these days is Instagram. Instagram has over 500 million daily active users. So, why shouldn't you leverage the power of the wide reach this platform offers? Using compelling photos, strategic hashtags, and publishing at the right time is a great way to build an Instagram following for your e-commerce store. The idea is to understand the importance of organic Instagram presents by increasing your engagement with the followers you have. So, it is not just about posting photos or content, but it is also about engaging with your target audience. The more you engage with them, the greater the chances that they will convert into paying customers.

Some of the simplest ways to engage with your target audience on Instagram is by running contests, going behind the scenes, or showcasing product development. Don't forget to experiment with various Instagram features like stories, IGTV, or even the different challenges that keep popping up. Keep the Instagram page light, friendly, fun, entertaining, and quirky. Don't make the content serious, brisk, and business-like. Instead, try to leverage the power of social media to increase the online visibility of your business.

Launching A Facebook Store

Facebook might not be the only social media platform available these days, but it certainly is a platform you cannot afford to overlook. The simplest way to make the most of Facebook is by launching a Facebook store. It is a great way to market your e-commerce store online. You can make sales via a Facebook store. You can also integrate this store with your Shopify store, so you don't have to maintain any separate inventory. Creating a Facebook store is a straightforward process. By placing a Facebook store tab on your business page, you can direct the users to purchase whatever products they liked directly from the Facebook profile. Instead of opening your website. The Facebook store app is an excellent and affordable way to increase your business exposure because of the large audience base that Facebook offers. Facebook stores can help increase new sales, increases the engagement potential with your customers, and belts plenty of brand awareness and recognition.

Wishlist Reminders

Don't forget to send wish list reminder emails to your subscriber list. The wish list reminder is quite similar to an email you would send an abandoned cart user. The purpose of both these emails is to convince them to shop or to nudge them toward making a purchase, instead of abandoning the cart altogether. As long as the user shows intent to buy, that is all you need to send a wish list email. Most of the online shopping apps tend to send notifications or emails in the form of wish list reminders. Is there an item on sale that's been included in several wish lists? Is the item selling out? Has it been a while since someone has reviewed their wish list? Well, if the answer is yes to all these questions, then it is time to send a quick wish list reminder. At times, users tend to forget about their carts after a while. Gently remind them, the best way to do it is by sending an email. Also, it might be the only push the user needs to become a paying customer.

Email Campaigns

In the previous chapter, you were given different tips you can follow to grow your email subscriber list. However, all those email addresses will do your business no good unless you use them effectively to market your e-commerce store. Businesses should regularly send valuable emails to all the subscribers on their email list. There are different occasions where sending an email is the ideal way to show that you appreciate your subscribers and the support they have shown towards your business. The simplest way to do this is by sending a welcome email as soon as a user makes a purchase. Don't forget to send regular newsletters alerting all your subscribers about new products, tips to use existing products, discounts, new offers, or any other news that is deemed appropriate for them. You can also use emails to send exclusive gifts or promo codes to all your subscribers. You can also share relevant content with all your customers to ensure that they make the most of their purchases. As long as the content is valuable to your target audience, don't hesitate to hit send. However, don't go overboard with all these emails. Ensure that you don't send more than one newsletter every week. If you bombard your subscribers with emails, they will quickly unsubscribe.

Avoid Poor Design

If your e-commerce store isn't well designed or is poorly designed, you will quickly lose more customers than you gain. A poorly designed site not only looks untrustworthy, but it often uses confusing navigation, offers an unclear value proposition, and uses the barely legible font. As stressed in the previous chapters, the design of your website is quintessential. When it comes to an e-commerce business. Since you don't have a physical storefront that your target audience can visit, your e-commerce store acts as the storefront. Spend sufficient time and don't rush into web designing. Shopify is an incredibly simple platform to use. As long as you're willing to dedicate the required time and effort, you can design a professional-looking website with little or no technical skills.

Keep in mind that regardless of how wonderful all the products offered on your website are, it doesn't make any sense if the users don't find your website engaging or appealing. First impressions matter a lot when it comes to online business. Therefore, make sure that the overall look of your website is pleasing and easy on the eyes.

Content Marketing

If you want to improve the ranking of your e-commerce store in search engine results or want to connect with your customers regularly, then consider blogging. If you are already churning out content, then try featuring it on a blog present on your online store. However, there are different ways in which you can do content marketing, which isn't necessarily restricted to creating a blog. You can also guest post on different websites or blogs to build awareness and create backlinks to your website. You can start a podcast featuring guest speakers. If you want, you can also create long-form content in the form of books and guides that your target audience will find helpful.

Use User-Generated Content

Generating social proof has become incredibly important in today's online world. The simplest way to do this is by using user-generated content. Whenever prospective customers view that others, just like them, are purchasing products from your website regularly, it increases their confidence in your business. One of the most effective ways to use user-generated content is by asking customers to post pictures where they are using the products you sell. For instance, if you sell clothes or shoes, you can encourage your customers to post pictures on their social media accounts wearing your products and tagging your business. It is not as customer reviews and testimonials that help improve your social proof, but even this simple tactic will work.

Personalization Matters

When it comes to increasing your online sales, personalization is a rather effective tactic. By using behavioral data, you can serve personalized experiences to all your visitors. Not a lot of businesses are aware of this tactic. So, try to make the most of it today. You can also use location to personalize or curate an experience that specifically caters to customers. Situated in a specific part of the world. For instance, if your website sells bathing suits, then ensure that you offer discounts and deals right before spring sets in. It could also happen that someone situated in Southern California might be looking for bathing suits during October, while those situated in Maine will probably look for winter wear.

Reward Loyal Customers

It is not just important to gain new customers, but you must also hold onto your loyal ones. Your loyal customers are the brand advocates you get free of charge. If you are doing a good job and have a loyal customer base, don't forget to appreciate them. Also, let them know you appreciate their continued support and association. There are various ways in which you can reward loyal customers or even big spenders by creating customer loyalty programs. You can give them extra incentives whenever they make a purchase or always give them priority access during offers running on your platform. Everyone likes to feel special and exclusive. When you give your loyal customers exclusive treatment, the chances are that they will stay loyal will increase.

Keep in mind that you're the only one that can decide how, when, and for what you wish to reward you, customers. For instance, you might come up with a point-based program on your online store, where certain points will be credited to a user's account whenever he makes a purchase. After collecting a predetermined number of points, the user can redeem them on any subsequent purchase he makes. You can also offer limited-time offers, free shipping, or other simple freebies to thank the loyal customers for their continued business.

By following the simple tips given in this chapter, you can improve the online visibility, traffic, and even sales your business makes. That said, keep in mind that it takes consistent time and effort to obtain the desired results from these marketing tactics. Learn to be patient, carefully monitor the results, and keep changing tactics according to the needs of your business.

Chapter 12: Shipping and Tax Rates

Unfortunately, if you're selling physical products, the work isn't over until the item is shipped to the customer, and the customer is happy. Taking the time to properly setup you're shipping and getting yourself prepared for the shipping process will help you streamline the process a bit. The ideal situation is that you will offer as many shipping options as possible for customer to choose from. In this manner, they can receive items at the best prices or the most opportune times.

Manual Shipping Rates

Manual shipping rates are flat rates applied to each product. After setting a manual rate, the customer will immediately know the cost of shipping, and you can ultimately ship the product out in any manner you choose if it reaches the customer. I would try to mention the expected shipment times to help customers out.

The advantage of this method is that you don't have to weigh each item, but the disadvantages are plentiful. Not only are the customers not able to customize how they want an item shipped (what if they need it quicker?), but they may also be taken aback if your shipping charge is much higher than it needs to be. If customers order multiple items, your fixed rate may not consider the size of the box required to ship them all at once. In general, it's not the best method to use.

The biggest disadvantage is that you may estimate poorly. Should the cost of shipping extend past the fixed rate you've set, then you will have to make up the cost difference on your own. This is fine if you build the price of shipping and materials into product prices, but you need to be diligent about how you price things.

If you only sell one line of product, and they're all practically the same size and weight, this option may be viable. If it isn't, you should offer shipping options to your customer.

Shopify USPS Shipping

Like eBay and PayPal, Shopify has a deal with the USPS that allows you to purchase labels at a discounted rate and print them off at home. Because you are most likely selling products that range from small to large, light to heavy, this is typically going to be the best method. All you need to do for your products is setup a weight, possibly slightly higher than the actual weight to accommodate for the packing materials and handling.

When the customer checks out, they can choose from several USPS options that allow them to pay more for quicker service. Shopify is automatically going to take the size and weight of your package into consideration and not allow them to order first-class mail when it's inappropriate, so there's no worries about getting underpaid for your shipping costs if your weights are correct. Additionally, the discounted rates (based on which tier of Shopify you use) will save you money. If you're a high-volume seller, and we all aim for that, then the Professional Plan's reduced rates will save you a healthy chunk of change over a period.

Other Carriers

You can also provide the option of other carriers for your customers, including UPS and FedEx, among others. Using the shipping setup in the settings, you'll be able to incorporate shipping APIs that allows these to be calculated much like the USPS costs are calculated. There is no discount involved with Shopify and these carriers, but if you have a business account with UPS, for example, your discount will still apply. Unfortunately, this is only available if you're a Professional member, which if you remember costs $299 per month. For high-volume sellers, it's worth having these additional options.

Fulfilment and Dropshipping

We've mentioned dropshipping briefly, but we'll cover this in greater detail later. This may be the best possible shipping method as the products aren't even in your possession or purchased by you until they are already sold to the customer!

There is also fulfilment shipping, which is similar in the idea that you're not the one handling the shipping, but unlike dropshipping, you already purchased the items, and now you're having them stored with a company that will ship them for you once they sell. This method may provide better profits than normal dropshipping, but you're still investing in the product and the fulfilment company's time. The ideal situation is to find a local fulfilment service where you can have products brought to without much fuss.

Shipping Settings

Now that we've covered the options for shipping, we must go through the process of setting it up. We ran through this briefly during the "Settings" part of the Shopify interface, so you may already be familiar with this if you took the time to explore.

Navigate to your "Settings" page and click on "Shipping."

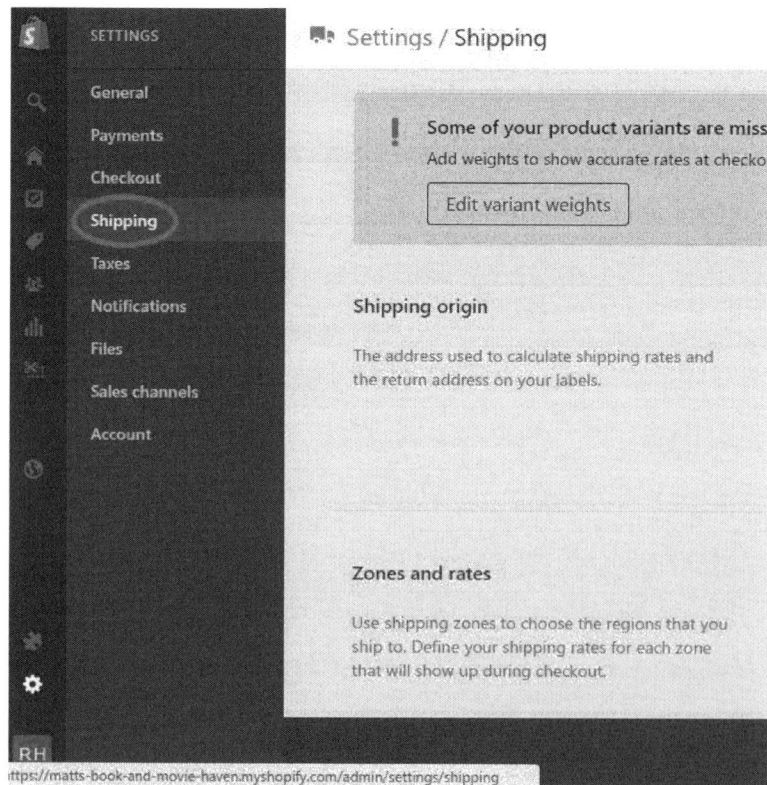

On this page, you'll see several things that you can adjust. This includes:

- Shipping Origin – This is the return address. Typically, it will be your home address unless you have a dedicated business location. If you do not want your home address on the label, then you can always open a PO Box at your local post office to avoid this. Do not use a fake address.

- Zones and rates – Here you can setup your shipping zones and rates. This includes the ability to limit shipping to certain parts of the world. By default, everything is included, so it may be wise to adjust if you don't aim to offer international shipping. Within the manual shipping rates.

- Label format – Next, you'll see the label format. If you're using special printers or labels, you can adjust this to fit your needs. If you're using a laser or inkjet printer that's standard and just taping on labels, then leave it at the default.

- Packages – If you have a selection of boxes you use for your shipments, inserting these sizes will help minimize the amount of time inputting this information for products later.

- Additional Shipping Methods – This is where you setup methods other than calculated USPS rates.

Shipping the Product

After an order is made, Shopify will notify you (unless you disabled notification), and they will give you the option to print out a shipping label. If you're using the standard calculated shipping, the label will default to match the information you've entered for calculated shipping. You can adjust this as needed. Always be sure your measurements and weights are correct.

To ship, you'll need a few things:

- *Boxes or bubble mailers* of multiple sizes that are appropriate for the products you stock. If you only have a few items for sale, you can hold off on buying in bulk, but once you begin moving product, you really need to keep some standard packaging materials on hand to speed up the process.

- *Padding,* such as bubble wrap and newspaper. Packing peanuts are becoming less common, and it is advised to avoid them as many customers find them inconsiderate to the environment.

- *Shipping tape.* Ideally, it will be clear. This way, if you're printing off paper labels and taping them to the box, you can tape over them a bit without it obstructing the information. Keep in mind that you're not supposed to tape over the barcodes. Nothing usually happens if you do, but it's technically discouraged by the USPS.

- *Printer* for printing labels.

- *Paper or label paper.* Label paper has adhesive back that means you can just peel and stick it to the box once it's printed. Once a product is labeled, you can take it to the post office or you can login at USPS and schedule a pickup.

If working with third-party carriers, check with them to ensure you're following all their guidelines. These companies will almost always offer home pickup as well. If you're working with fulfilment services, Shopify and the service will help you set this up in a way that will automate the shipments thereafter.

Shipping Rates and Order Fulfillment

To set your shipping rates, from your control panel, click on "Shipping." Input whatever locations and rates that you want but the easiest is to have two – a home country rate and then a "Rest of the World" rate.

Further down the page, there are options for adding Drop Shipping or Order Fulfillment. These are not Shopify services and are run by third parties – some of them very recognizable names. This is a great way of selling products across the whole world without needing to send packages yourself. You send the drop shipping company a load of your products and they do everything

for you – storage of stock, packaging and posting. And, because Shopify will integrate easily with these services, your sales can be handled by the other company without you getting involved in the order.

Tax Rates

If you earn over a certain threshold in most countries, there are tax or VAT systems in place. If tax must be added to orders, click on "Tax" in the main admin panel and input the correct tax amount in the box for "Country Tax Rate."

This will then appear on invoices and you will be able to see the tax you collected in your sales reports. If you don't have to collect any tax, this value can just be set as zero.

To see tax reports, click on "Reports" and then on "Tax Rate."

Chapter 13: Mistakes to Avoid

Are you just getting started with an e-commerce business? At times, the entire process can be a little overwhelming, and creating your first venture will seem like a daunting task. However, with practice, it will all get easier. Making mistakes is an elementary aspect of learning. Well, you don't necessarily have to make mistakes to learn. You can learn a lot from the mistakes of others too. Let us look at some of the most common Shopify mistakes and how to avoid them.

Using the Default Settings

Concentrating on SEO should be your priority if you want to increase the visibility of your online store or the products you offer. To increase your SEO ratings, avoid using the default settings for Meta tags. So, every page, blog post, and product must be inserted manually into the Meta tags for your website's SEO. Whenever you edit a product or a page, open the Edit Website SEO option at the bottom of your page and then click on the edit Meta Information. If you fail to do this, then the first 160 characters from your webpage, collection, or product page will be set as the default title. SEO is not just important to improve your online visibility, but also offers a better user experience.

Lack of a Uniform Theme

All the different colors present in the Shopify theme must match your store. Therefore, always double-check the color consistency. For instance, any clickable links to your website must be of the same color. Carefully go through the different configurations and website settings to ensure that all the vital information is displayed consistently. To create a consistent shopping experience for all your customers, carefully review the selections of your e-commerce store.

No Branding

The reputation of your business in the market is conveyed through its logo. Even if your e-commerce store is launched on a wide scale, your brand might not amass a huge following if it doesn't have a logo. What is the first thing that passes through to your mind when you view a bright yellow M? You might be reminded of McDonald's. So, never belittle the power of branding, and always have a logo to create quick business recognition. If you don't think you have the required skills to design the logo, don't hesitate to hire some professional help.

Improper Contact Information

The about us or the contact page is quite important for any e-commerce store or website. It is one page you cannot afford to overlook if you want to be a successful e-commerce store owner. The About Us page is your business's primary introduction to its potential customers. This page talks about the vision, mission, and value statement of your business and its unique selling point. It must also include contact information like phone number, email, actress, fax number, and a PO box address wherever applicable.

Checkout Page Matters

There are many customization options available for checkout pages on Shopify. Therefore, always check the checkout pages of the website before you launch the store. When you use the website or the e-commerce store from a customer's perspective, you will get a better insight into the things that work and don't work in your favor. It is quintessential that the checkout process on your e-commerce store is easy and hassle-free. Ideally, the look of the checkout page must be similar to the other pages of your e-commerce store. Also, ensure that the font used is similar throughout the website. The checkout page should not seem like a misplaced extension of your e-commerce Shopify store.

Limit the Font Selection

Shopify offers a variety of fonts, and finding the right kind of font for your e-commerce store might seem a little daunting. Before you select a font, always shortlist at least two or three fonts and then find one that goes well with your brand and store name. You can create a variety of looks using a single font type due to the various options available, like bold, letter spacing, thin, italics, and regular styles. If you want to lend a polished and well-defined look to your e-commerce store, then the font style needs to be consistent across the website. You cannot use one font style for a page and then change it for the other pages. Also, if you use multiple fonts on a single page, it makes the website seem cluttered.

Don't Overlook the Soft Launch

Before you line up for a grand online opening, opt for a soft launch of the online store. In a soft launch, introduce your website or e-commerce store only to a limited number of people. Before this site goes live for everyone, conduct a soft launch. When you do this, you will get a rough idea about the different features of your site that work and don't work in its favor. Use the feedback you receive from a soft launch, and you can make any required changes before the website goes live. A soft launch is like a select screening of a movie before its actual release.

Not Offering Multiple Payment Options

If you want to enhance the value of sales and the number of customers your online store gathers, then you need to offer a variety of payment options. Never restrict yourself to a single payment gateway and include a couple of options. If you end up offering only one or two payment options, not all your potential customers need to use the same payment gateways.

Lack of a Marketing Plan

You cannot make the most of the benefits offered by Shopify unless you have a sound marketing strategy in place. It helps provide guidelines about your target audience, selling tactics, business coach, or even the promotional setup. A good marketing plan provides a detailed overview of not just your ideal target audience but the selling cycle too. A simple way to piece together a marketing strategy is to define your brand's message and the USP, your target audience, various marketing tactics, and the different goals you have in mind.

Lack of Optimization

The landing pages are a bit different from the usual pages on your business website. A landing page serves a specific purpose. The purpose is defined by the source that leads your target audience to the website. Usually, a Landing Page helps generate leads and boost a specific call to action while providing more information about the product, service offered, and any item that is sold. Your landing pages need to be thoroughly optimized, must direct the user in the right direction, and needs to perform a specific action. An ideal landing page must guide you, visitors, capture necessary email addresses, cross-sell, or even upsell, and generate some interest in whatever your business offers.

Overlooking First-Time Visitors

Never underestimate the power of a good first impression. First impressions matter a lot, mainly when it comes to selling and online selling, in particular. One mistake you must try to avoid at all costs is not putting your best foot forward while welcoming a first-time visitor to your e-commerce store. The first impression your store manages to make with them will determine whether they will proceed and make a sale or exit the website. A couple of factors you can consider to create a powerful first impression is the message your landing page of the website provides, the color scheme, the pop-ups you use, and your engagement tactics. If your website is attractive, makes the visitor feel valued, or offers very valuable information and deals, the chances of conversion will increase.

Lack of Awareness

You cannot become a successful business owner if you are unsure of your target audience. Before you think about launching your business, spend some time to answer the question, who is my target audience carefully? Regardless of how wonderful your idea is, you cannot successfully sell it if there are no takers. Therefore, you must be thoroughly aware of your ideal customer. An ideal customer is a person who is most likely to grab any product or service your website offers. When you have sufficient clarity about your target audience, it helps you select the right products and concentrate on a personalized and customized marketing strategy.

Avoid PPC Ads

Pay per click or PPC ads are an incredible way to generate more leads and increase conversions. However, plenty of people tend to overlook or underestimate the overall power PPC ads offer. It doesn't take much time or effort to launch a successful PPC campaign. If you are in it for the long run, then you cannot overlook the importance of PPC ad campaigns. A PPC campaign enables you to generate traffic and leads more quickly than organic SEO traffic. It also helps you check and change the ad budget, depending on the ROI. When your PPC campaign is well planned, you can reduce the cost per click. Also, you can use a PPC ad for A/B testing and shutdown a campaign when you don't get the desired results.

You need plenty of knowledge and understanding before you can launch a successful PPC ad campaign. If you're just getting started with Shopify, there are a couple of apps you can use to integrate PPC ad campaigns with your e-commerce store. The most popular options include Google ads and Google shopping. You can also use adNabu or other third-party apps to create and integrate a PPC ad campaign with your e-commerce Shopify story.

Ignoring Accounting

The importance of accounting can never be overlooked. Keep in mind that you are starting a business, and, as with any other business, keeping track of your accounts matters a lot. Bookkeeping, taxes, invoicing and keeping track of expenses matter a lot. If you don't have a proper record of all this, then you might end up over or underestimating the profits you make. Also, to stay on top of all the taxes payable, you need to have solid accounts in place. If you hate to run into any legal hassle, then never overlook the importance of detailed accounting. There are various online and accounting automation apps and software you can use to keep track of all the accounts. If you want, you can go the old school route and maintain the accounts in a journal. If you don't have the knack for accounting, then you can hire a professional to help you with all this.

Conclusion

Today multi-channel selling is popular, which entails making a sale across multiple platforms. Do not just wait for the customers to visit your website, rather attract them using platforms such as Facebook, Twitter, and Instagram. You should not be ignorant of such trends because they play an important role in connecting you with customers.

Also, you are encouraged to do a proper assessment when seeking to set up a successful Shopify store. This is where you identify a market niche. You need to identify the products that you will be dealing with, which are, those you know have a broad market and ensure customers will be willing and able to buy them online.

For instance, health and fitness products have gained significant popularity in the market. It is common to come across blogs encouraging people to be attentive with what they are eating and to exercise regularly. This increased awareness of health issues has created a market for health and fitness products. Also, there is a growing market for consumer electronics such as personal computers, laptops, smartphones, and TVs, among others. Furthermore, Millennials have created a broad market for beauty and fashion products. You should take advantage of these markets and target certain customers, provide suitable content, and give people offers that will attract them to your store.

You have been provided with an extensive discussion on how to find reliable suppliers. It has been noted that not all businesses you come across will be legitimate wholesalers, you must take your time in researching for suitable suppliers.

An aspect that you be aware of is ensuring you are selling your products at as low a price as possible. To ensure you are dealing with competitive prices and making profits at the same time, you will need to look for legitimate wholesalers or suppliers who will give you suitable market prices. From there you will be able to sell at a mark-up price.

Be cautious of the retailers who pretend to be wholesalers. They will be selling their products at a higher cost than wholesalers. When you engage with such suppliers, you will end up selling at higher prices than the competitors.

Another aspect you must compare is local and international suppliers. For instance, cost, quality, and the customers' social class will determine whether to deal with a local or international supplier. You can also come across ideal suppliers through referral, Google search, attending trade shows, or contacting manufacturers.

As noted, you need a marketing plan to succeed in differentiating your brand. A marketing plan is important because it enables you to carry out calculated and assessed actions.

When you engage in marketing planning, you get the opportunity to think and become more conversant with aspects relating to the target customers. Look at the marketing plan as a strategic plan that informs you of customer needs and wants. Also, you get to learn how to attract them, reach them, and tell them what they want to hear. It will then be possible to engage them, follow up, and convert them into customers, which in turn will increase your sales.

Related is the aspect of increasing your sales funnel through Facebook marketing. You were guided on how to reach maximum customer value. If you attain this, it means you have managed to attain a class of loyal customers and you can retain your customers.

Printed in Great Britain
by Amazon